How to Love Me

How to Love Me

The LOVERS' BOOK *of* QUESTIONS | ALI DAVIS

STERLING

New York / London
www.sterlingpublishing.com

STERLING and the distinctive Sterling logo are registered trademarks of Sterling Publishing Co., Inc.

Library of Congress Cataloging-in-Publication Data Available
10 9 8 7 6 5 4 3 2 1

Produced by Hollan Publishing, Inc.
100 Cummings Center, Suite 125G
Beverly, MA 01915
www.hollanpub.com
HOLLAN   © 2007 by Hollan Publishing, Inc.

Published by Sterling Publishing Co., Inc.
387 Park Avenue South, New York, NY 10016

Distributed in Canada by Sterling Publishing
c/o Canadian Manda Group, 165 Dufferin Street
Toronto, Ontario, Canada M6K 3H6
Distributed in the United Kingdom by GMC Distribution Services
Castle Place, 166 High Street, Lewes, East Sussex, England BN7 1XU
Distributed in Australia by Capricorn Link (Australia) Pty. Ltd.
P.O. Box 704, Windsor, NSW 2756, Australia

Sterling ISBN-13: 978-1-4027-4918-6
    ISBN-10: 1-4027-4918-X

For information about custom editions, special sales, premium and corporate purchases, please contact Sterling Special Sales Department at 800-805-5489 or specialsales@sterlingpub.com.

Cover and interior design by John Barnett

Contents

Introduction

"Love looks not with the eyes but with the mind."

A MIDSUMMER NIGHT'S DREAM
(I, I, 234)

So you've met the person of your dreams, or at least a really "dreamy" person. You've moved beyond that initial phase of attraction: the admiring glance across the room, the affectionate gaze across a candlelit table for two, even the seductive stare across a shared pillow. Are you ready to take things to the next level?

If you want the kind of love that Shakespeare writes about—the kind that runs deeper than the flesh and satisfies you in ways you never imagined, then it's time to come clean and bare all! The better you know yourself and how you want to be—make that *need* to be—loved, the better your love life will be. It's time to start asking yourself some difficult questions: What do *I* really want in a relationship? How can *I* make the relationship I'm in more satisfying? What do *I* need from my partner? *How to Love Me* is filled with hundreds of leading questions like these— questions that force you to look inward and let your deepest desires be known.

When you've boldly and truthfully tackled the questions that follow, it's time to let the man or woman in your life know what you're all about. You can simply hand the book over, play Truth or Dare, or leave it lying around enticingly opened to the relevant pages. Whatever you choose, I hope it leads to some interesting discussion and lots of fun along the way.

How to Love Me will help you stay true to who you are and what you want, and could even bring a whole new level of satisfaction to your relationship.

Now it's time to indulge in a little self-exploration. If you weren't sure who you were before you bought this book, you're about to find out …

The Big Ones

chapter 1

The Intangibles

Love is …
☐ spiritual ☐ emotional ☐ chemical ☐ an illusion

Love means …
☐ being willing to change for someone
☐ understanding that you can't change your partner

Each person on earth has only one true love.
☐ true ☐ false

I believe in fate and destiny.
☐ true ☐ false

It is possible to be in love with more than one person at the same time.
☐ true ☐ false

Having sex and making love are two different things.
☐ true ☐ false

Relationships …
☐ shouldn't be hard if you're truly in love ☐ take a lot of work

It's wrong to date someone you don't think you're in love with or going to fall in love with.
☐ true ☐ false

If I had to choose between the two, I'd rather be …
  ☐ the one who is loved but not in love
  ☐ the one who is in love, but not loved

Love conquers all.
  ☐ absolutely   ☐ don't be ridiculous

It's possible to gradually grow attracted to a mate you're not attracted to.
  ☐ true   ☐ false

Over time, it is possible to fall in love with a partner you previously have not been in love with.
  ☐ true   ☐ false

Good relationships are just about aligning your quirks and flaws with someone else's.
  ☐ true   ☐ false

It's important to be friends with my mate.
  ☐ true   ☐ false

If I had to choose one, I'd pick …
  ☐ lifelong love   ☐ lifelong financial security

In any relationship, there is always one person who is more in love.
  ☐ true   ☐ false

Sex without love is …
  ☐ good clean fun   ☐ naughty dirty fun   ☐ wrong
  ☐ a workout   ☐ not as much fun as sex with love

I'd be willing to sacrifice anything for someone I loved.
  ☐ yes   ☐ no

I expect someone who loves me to be willing to sacrifice anything.
  ☐ yes   ☐ no

When you meet the person you're going to spend the rest of your life with, you just know.
  ☐ true   ☐ false

To me, the most taboo sex act is:

_____

The worst crime in the world is:

_____

The best thing you could possibly do for someone else is:

_____

I believe that the world is basically a good place.
☐ true ☐ false

TANGIBLES

I'd rather …
☐ be with the wrong person than be alone
☐ be alone than with the wrong person

I want to get married someday.
☐ true ☐ false

I want to get married in the next five years.
☐ true ☐ false

I want to get married in the next two years.
☐ true ☐ false

I'm really only interested in a relationship that has marriage potential.
☐ yes ☐ no

It's okay to have sex before marriage.
☐ yes ☐ no

Sex is …
☐ the most important thing ☐ important
☐ not important

If I discovered I was pregnant and I wasn't married, I'd:

_____

_____

If I discovered my son or daughter were gay, I'd:

_____

_____

The thing I like most about the idea of settling down with someone is:

_____

_____

My biggest fear about getting into a committed relationship is:

_____

_____

If I wanted kids and discovered I couldn't have them, I'd:

_____

_____

If I wanted kids and discovered my mate couldn't have them, I'd:

_____

_____

Anal sex:
　☐ yes ☐ no ☐ only on special occasions

Pornography is …
　☐ not something I can tolerate, ever ☐ fine, as long as you don't watch
　or look at it while I'm around ☐ fine, as long as it's something we're
　enjoying together ☐ really beginning to take up a lot of space in my
　hard drive

It's normal for physical attraction to fade over the course of a relationship.
　☐ true ☐ false

I have met my partner's parents.
　☐ yes ☐ no

If the above answer is yes: I have concerns about my partner's parents'
relationship.
　☐ yes ☐ no

Condoms/dental dams:
　☐ mandatory ☐ mandatory until we're in a monogamous dating
　relationship ☐ mandatory until we're married ☐ mandatory for
　intercourse, but not oral sex ☐ I prefer to use them ☐ I don't usually
　use them ☐ I don't use them at all

I've been tested for STDs …
　☐ once or twice ☐ after my last partner before you
　☐ since I started seeing you ☐ never

We should talk about STDs ...
- [ ] because that's what sensible adults do
- [ ] because I think I might have one [ ] because I know I have one
- [ ] because I think you might have one [ ] I would rather do anything than talk about STDs

The idea of a threesome is ...
- [ ] exciting, and I'd like to try it [ ] exciting, but only as a fantasy
- [ ] something that makes me feel jealous [ ] out of the question

Dating someone of another race would be ...
- [ ] not that big a deal [ ] something I'd be nervous about
- [ ] exotic [ ] out of the question

Pain during sex is ...
- [ ] not something I'm into [ ] okay, as long as it's mild and mutual
- [ ] essential

The Dealbreakers

SPIRITUALITY

I consider myself:
- ☐ religious ☐ deeply religious ☐ spiritual, but not religious
- ☐ agnostic ☐ searching ☐ atheist ☐ not sure

I would be able to spend my life with someone with radically different spiritual views.
- ☐ yes ☐ no

Other faiths are just as valid as mine.
- ☐ yes ☐ no ☐ certain ones yes, certain ones no

I am concerned about my mate and I being able to spend eternity together.
- ☐ yes ☐ no

I am concerned that my mate's faith might come before our relationship.
- ☐ yes ☐ no

People who are religious are clinging to old superstitions.
- ☐ true ☐ false

It is possible to have faith and believe in evolution.
- ☐ yes ☐ no

I could get married to someone of another religion.
  ☐ absolutely ☐ absolutely not ☐ yes, but my family would be upset
  ☐ yes, with some reservations ☐ only if they converted
  ☐ date, yes; marry, no

I believe that …
  ☐ we are here to enjoy this world, now
  ☐ we are here to sacrifice for greater rewards later

Religion …
  ☐ causes more suffering than good
  ☐ causes more good than suffering

I believe that many organized religions could benefit by gaining more of a sense of humor.
  ☐ true ☐ false

I feel better if I start each day with prayer or meditation.
  ☐ true ☐ false

I prefer to start my meals with grace.
  ☐ true ☐ false

I believe that proselytizing is a key part of my faith.
  ☐ true ☐ false

I would feel comfortable in a long-term relationship with someone who would like to convert me to his or her faith.
  ☐ true ☐ false

All or most faiths are praying to the same thing that they call by different names.
  ☐ true ☐ false

POLITICS

I consider myself …
  ☐ green ☐ liberal ☐ ultra-liberal ☐ moderate ☐ conservative
  ☐ neocon ☐ ultra-conservative ☐ libertarian
  ☐ I take it on an issue-by-issue basis ☐ I don't follow politics
  ☐ other _____

My feelings about politics are …
  ☐ passionate ☐ strong ☐ average
  ☐ I'm skipping this section

I would be able to spend my life with someone who had different political views than mine.
   ☐ yes ☐ no

I would be able to listen to my partner talk about his or her political views during an entire cocktail party without once rolling my eyes.
   ☐ yes ☐ no

I would be able to go to sleep at night next to someone who voted differently than I did in the last U.S. Presidential election.
   ☐ yes ☐ no ☐ never!

I have …
   ☐ taken part in demonstrations ☐ acted for a political cause
   ☐ donated substantially to political causes ☐ never done any of those

When it comes to the news, I …
   ☐ like to keep informed ☐ just don't have time for it
   ☐ find it too depressing ☐ am a complete news junkie

It's okay if my partner cares much more about politics than I do.
   ☐ yes ☐ no

It's okay if my partner cares much less about politics than I do.
   ☐ yes ☐ no

To me, the most important political issue right now is …
   ☐ the environment ☐ the population explosion ☐ terrorism
   ☐ poverty ☐ family values ☐ racism ☐ gay rights
   ☐ the economy ☐ globalization ☐ education
   ☐ other _____

DRUGS

My general attitude toward drugs is …
   ☐ the more, the merrier! ☐ occasional use is okay, as long as you don't form any habits ☐ I don't have a problem with experimenting
   ☐ pot and alcohol are okay, hard drugs are not ☐ alcohol is okay, drugs are not ☐ no drugs, no alcohol, ever

When I drink, it's …
   ☐ usually just one or two with dinner ☐ usually several, at parties
   ☐ usually until I'm out of control

Drinking to the point of vomiting or a hangover is …
☐ something I do most weekends ☐ something I did in high school or college ☐ something I don't approve of

You holding my hair while I vomit is …
☐ a loving gesture ☐ a sign that the relationship may be over

I've slept with someone while drunk that I wouldn't have slept with completely sober.
☐ true ☐ false

Knowing that you had slept with someone while drunk that you wouldn't have slept with completely sober would make me feel …
☐ like I couldn't trust you
☐ not bad—we all screw up sometimes
☐ uncomfortable ☐ a certain kinship with you

Hallucinogens are …
☐ mind-expanding ☐ harmless ☐ dangerous

Drinking a cocktail or a beer or two every day is …
☐ normal ☐ a bad pattern

Smoking a joint every day is …
☐ unacceptable ☐ a little too much ☐ something that's okay when you're in college, but not for real adults ☐ my usual

I could date someone who doesn't drink at all or drinks much less than I do.
☐ true ☐ false

I could date someone who drinks quite a bit more than I do.
☐ true ☐ false

I could date someone who doesn't do drugs at all or does much less than I do.
☐ true ☐ false

I could date someone who does more drugs than I do.
☐ true ☐ false

Past experimentation with drugs is okay.
☐ true ☐ false

I could date a recovering drug addict.
☐ true ☐ false

I could date a recovering alcoholic.
☐ true   ☐ false

I am a recovering drug addict or alcoholic.
☐ yes   ☐ no   ☐ I'm thinking about entering a program

Drinking before sex:
☐ relaxes me   ☐ I can take it or leave it
☐ shouldn't happen at all   ☐ needs to happen every time
☐ is okay some of the time, but I'd worry if it were every time

Smoking pot before sex:
☐ relaxes me   ☐ I can take it or leave it
☐ shouldn't happen at all   ☐ needs to happen every time
☐ is okay some of the time, but I'd worry if it were every time

CHEATING

I've been cheated on before.
☐ yes   ☐ no   ☐ I never had proof, but I'm pretty sure it happened

I'd be okay with you going to see a stripper with your friends.
☐ true   ☐ false

I'd be okay with you going to see a stripper with me.
☐ true   ☐ false

Strippers at a bachelor or bachelorette party don't count.
☐ true   ☐ false

Flirting with someone else at a party is …
☐ exciting   ☐ harmless   ☐ creepy   ☐ cheating

Giving a back massage or foot massage to someone else is cheating.
☐ true   ☐ false

Kissing someone else is cheating.
☐ true   ☐ false

Flirting or chatting on sites like MySpace or Facebook is cheating.
☐ true   ☐ false

Cybersex is cheating.
☐ true   ☐ false

Mutual masturbation is cheating.
☐ true ☐ false

Oral sex is cheating.
☐ true ☐ false

If you did cheat, I'd rather …
☐ know ☐ not know

I'd be more upset by …
☐ a one-night stand, purely for sex
☐ a longtime close emotional attachment that never led to sex

Having sex with someone else is only cheating if we've had a talk and specifically agreed to be exclusive.
☐ true ☐ false

I expect our relationship to be exclusive once we start sleeping together.
☐ yes ☐ no

I expect our relationship to be exclusive once we've been dating for …
☐ six months ☐ three months ☐ a month
☐ one date ☐ it depends

Keeping in touch with ex-girlfriends or -boyfriends is a sign of …
☐ an ability to handle breakups maturely
☐ shadiness

I'd be willing to be a part of an open relationship.
☐ yes ☐ no
☐ over my dead body
☐ that's the only kind of relationship I'm considering right now

The worst consequence of cheating is:
☐ jealousy ☐ the lack of trust ☐ the risk of STDs
☐ other _____

I'd be able to forgive you if you had a one-night stand.
☐ yes ☐ no ☐ I don't know

I'd be able to forgive you if you had an affair.
☐ yes ☐ no ☐ I don't know

If I caught you cheating, I'd expect to have payback sex with someone else.
☐ yes ☐ no ☐ I'd at least let you think I would

It's okay for you to spend the day with an ex.

☐ yes ☐ no ☐ depends on the ex in question

If I could choose one ex you'd never spend time with again, it would be:

_____

It's okay for you to hang out alone with a friend who's the same gender as I am.

☐ yes ☐ no

It's okay for you to hang out alone with a really hot friend who's the same gender as I am.

☐ yes ☐ no

In all honesty, I get jealous when you:

_____

Making a list of five celebrities that each of us gets a free pass to sleep with is ...

☐ fun ☐ inexplicable

And, by the way, my list is:

1. _____
2. _____
3. _____
4. _____
5. _____

KIDS

I want kids.

☐ no ☐ I'm not sure ☐ yes, one ☐ yes, two or three ☐ yes, several

I'm willing to commit to someone who doesn't want kids.

☐ yes ☐ no

I'm willing to commit to someone who wants kids.

☐ yes ☐ no

I'm willing to commit to someone who isn't sure.

☐ yes ☐ no

I'm willing to commit to someone who already has kids.

☐ yes ☐ no

I'm willing to commit to someone who already has kids and wants more with me.
☐ yes ☐ no

I'm willing to commit to someone who already has kids and doesn't want any more.
☐ yes ☐ no

I'm willing to live with kids from a past relationship.
☐ yes ☐ no

I would …
☐ prefer to adopt ☐ consider adoption
☐ not be willing to adopt

I'd be willing to take in a foster child.
☐ yes ☐ no

I'd be willing to foster or adopt an older child.
☐ yes ☐ no

I'd be willing to adopt a child of another race.
☐ yes ☐ no

Assuming we both have kids, I'd expect to spend holidays …
☐ all together ☐ with one side of the family or the other
☐ just as a couple ☐ we'll play it by ear each time.

If I have to err on one side or the other, I believe it's best to give kids a little too much …
☐ freedom ☐ discipline

Kids should only get an allowance if they earn it through chores.
☐ yes ☐ no

I believe it's more important to …
☐ focus on making us work as a couple
☐ focus on the kids

Divorce is not an option if kids are involved.
☐ true ☐ false

I expect to educate my kids …
☐ by home-school ☐ at a private school ☐ at a public school

I feel like I want or need to start having kids ...
☐ within ten years   ☐ within five years   ☐ within two years
☐ seriously, I don't want kids

I think it's okay for kids to start dating at age: _____

I think the best way to raise good kids is to:

_____

My Personal Dealbreakers

Clothing is a dealbreaker for me.
☐ yes   ☐ no

Intelligence is a dealbreaker for me.
☐ yes   ☐ no

Musical taste is a dealbreaker for me.
☐ yes   ☐ no

Sense of humor is a dealbreaker for me
☐ yes   ☐ no

Income is a dealbreaker for me.
☐ yes   ☐ no

Gift-giving is a dealbreaker for me.
☐ yes   ☐ no

A criminal record is a dealbreaker for me.
☐ yes   ☐ no

Education is a dealbreaker for me.
☐ yes   ☐ no

Grammar is a dealbreaker for me.
☐ yes   ☐ no

Physical activity is a dealbreaker for me.
☐ yes   ☐ no

Division of household chores is a dealbreaker for me.
☐ yes   ☐ no

Sex before marriage is a dealbreaker for me.
☐ yes ☐ no

Loving my home sports team is a dealbreaker for me.
☐ yes ☐ no

An aversion to pets is a dealbreaker for me.
☐ yes ☐ no

An allergy to pets is a dealbreaker for me.
☐ yes ☐ no

Height is a dealbreaker for me.
☐ yes ☐ no

Hair/baldness is a dealbreaker for me.
☐ yes ☐ no

Smoking is a dealbreaker for me.
☐ yes ☐ no

Oral sex is a dealbreaker for me.
☐ yes ☐ no

I think your parents may be a dealbreaker for me.
☐ no ☐ we should talk

A past marriage is a dealbreaker for me.
☐ yes ☐ no

The number of sex partners you've had may be a dealbreaker for me.
☐ yes ☐ no

A past encounter with prostitute is a dealbreaker for me.
☐ yes ☐ no

Multiple past encounters with prostitutes would be a dealbreaker for me.
☐ yes ☐ no

Personal hygiene is a dealbreaker for me.
☐ yes ☐ no

… And we should talk about that.
☐ yes ☐ no

The way someone laughs or smiles is a dealbreaker for me.
☐ yes ☐ no

Condom use is a dealbreaker for me.
☐ yes ☐ no

A past STD is a dealbreaker for me.
☐ yes ☐ no

An incurable STD like herpes is a dealbreaker for me.
☐ yes ☐ no

Quality of sex is a dealbreaker for me.
☐ yes ☐ no

… And we should talk about that.
☐ yes ☐ no

Frequency of sex is a dealbreaker for me.
☐ yes ☐ no

… And we should talk about that.
☐ yes ☐ no

No sex at all would be a dealbreaker for me.
☐ yes ☐ no

Your friends may be a dealbreaker for me.
☐ yes ☐ no

Gaining or losing a lot of weight would be a dealbreaker for me.
☐ yes ☐ no

I think one or more of your quirks or habits may be dealbreakers for me:

_____

_____

Another possible dealbreaker that you and I should talk about is:

_____

_____

My Relationship

chapter 3

My Satisfaction

I could use a little more…
- ☐ romance ☐ conversation ☐ help around the house
- ☐ passion ☐ friendship

If had to choose one, I'd choose …
- ☐ more time together ☐ more space

My general interest in sex is …
- ☐ high ☐ average ☐ low

I'd be more interested in sex if you:

_____

_____

My favorite part of sex is …
- ☐ kissing ☐ making out ☐ undressing each other
- ☐ oral sex ☐ intercourse ☐ cuddling afterwards
- ☐ other _____

In bed, I'd love you to pay more attention to …
- ☐ my breasts ☐ my ears ☐ my thighs ☐ my feet ☐ my neck
- ☐ my clitoris ☐ my penis ☐ another body part _____

I'd love more …
- ☐ cuddling ☐ kissing/making out ☐ quickies ☐ sex in general

My favorite way to kiss is:
☐ no tongue   ☐ light tongue   ☐ deep kissing with plenty of tongue

The best kiss you ever gave me was:

_____

My favorite time you and I had sex was:

_____

My favorite way to have an orgasm is …
☐ intercourse   ☐ oral sex   ☐ masturbation with my hand
☐ masturbation with your hand   ☐ masturbation with a vibrator
☐ other _____

I'm most likely to have an orgasm through …
☐ intercourse   ☐ oral sex   ☐ masturbation with my hand
☐ masturbation with your hand   ☐ masturbation with a vibrator
☐ other _____

The position in which it's easiest for me to experience orgasm is:

_____

I prefer sex …
☐ in the morning   ☐ at night   ☐ in the afternoon

I prefer sex to be …
☐ gentle   ☐ rough   ☐ it depends on my mood

I enjoy giving oral sex.
☐ true   ☐ false

I'd enjoy it more if you:

_____

I enjoy receiving oral sex.
☐ true   ☐ false

I'd enjoy it more if you:

_____

The thing I have the most difficulty with in bed is …
☐ communicating   ☐ performing cunnilingus   ☐ receiving cunnilingus
☐ performing fellatio   ☐ receiving fellatio   ☐ reaching orgasm
☐ other _____

You can help me with that by:

_____

Dirty talk is …
    ☐ hot ☐ gross ☐ silly ☐ essential

I'd like our foreplay to be …
    ☐ longer ☐ shorter

I'd like …
    ☐ to initiate sex more often ☐ for you to initiate sex more often

I enjoy wearing lingerie.
    ☐ true ☐ false

Sex outdoors:
    ☐ yes ☐ no

My Partner (That's You…)

I'm most attracted to you when you are:
    ☐ talking ☐ sleeping ☐ working out ☐ playing a sport
    ☐ performing ☐ cooking ☐ dancing
    ☐ other _____

My favorite thing about you is:
    ☐ your body ☐ your looks ☐ your intelligence ☐ your sense of
    humor
    ☐ your talent ☐ your ambition ☐ your values ☐ your stability
    ☐ your danger ☐ other _____

The thing I first noticed about you was:

_____

The thing that first attracted me to you was:

_____

At first I didn't like it, but now I love your:

_____

The proudest I've ever been of you was:

_____

The time I felt most taken care of by you was:

_____

I feel safest with you when:

_____

My favorite meal you make is:

_____

My favorite way to see you dressed is:

_____

Seeing you cry makes me feel …
  ☐ closer to you ☐ uncomfortable ☐ less respect for you

When you're jealous, it makes me feel …
  ☐ attractive and taken care of ☐ like you don't trust me

The thing I've learned about you that surprised me the most is:

_____

You don't know it, but I love it when you:

_____

 My favorite friend of yours is:

_____

I love watching you:

_____

You're at your best when you:

_____

You're funniest when you:

_____

My favorite little habit of yours is:

_____

My least favorite article of your clothing is:

_____

If I could replace or update one of your possessions, it would be:

_____

My favorite outfit of yours is:

_____

The thing I'd like to know about you the most is:

_____

I'm worried that I don't do this well enough for you:

_____

If money were no object, I'd give you:

_____

My favorite thing you do in the morning is:

_____

My least favorite thing you do in the morning is:

_____

My favorite thing you do before bed is:

_____

My least favorite thing you do before bed is:

_____

My favorite part of your body is your:

_____

The body part that you don't like but I secretly love is your:

_____

You're physically my type because …

_____
_____

Your personality fits my type because …

_____
_____

You're different than anyone else I've dated because …

_____
_____

I love it when I catch you:
   ☐ talking to yourself ☐ playing air guitar
   ☐ singing in the shower ☐ playing with a pet
   ☐ daydreaming
   ☐ other _____

When we're in public, I love it when you:

_____

_____

When we're in public, I dislike it when you:

_____

_____

When you're with your friends, I notice that you:

_____

_____

When we're alone, I notice that you:

_____

_____

The weirdest dream I've ever had about you is:

_____

_____

I think it means:

_____

_____

Three things about you that I love, but I'm not sure you know about are:
1. _____
2. _____
3. _____

I feel most confident around you when:

_____

_____

My favorite thing to do together is:

_____

_____

I get a little crush on you all over again when you:

_____

_____

A little habit you have that turns me off is:

_____

_____

The closest you've come to losing me was when you:

_____

_____

You think I love it, but I really just tolerate it:

_____

_____

I wish you knew how great you are at:

_____

I wish you would ask me more about:

_____

I wish you would talk more about:

_____

I wish I could see more of your:
 ☐ masculine side ☐ feminine side

The friend of yours I most admire: _____

The member of your family I feel most comfortable with: _____

The member of your family I think you're most like: _____

The member of your family I'd most like to improve my relationship with:

_____

… And here's how you can help with that:

_____

_____

My Wishes

The one thing I'd most like you to try in bed is:

_____

The place I'd most like to try having sex is:

_____

Food and sex …
 ☐ don't mix ☐ double your pleasure

The idea of hearing someone else having sex is …
    ☐ appealing   ☐ not appealing   ☐ out of the question   ☐ routine

The idea of being overheard while we have sex is…
    ☐ appealing   ☐ not appealing   ☐ out of the question   ☐ routine

The idea of seeing someone else have sex is …
    ☐ appealing   ☐ not appealing   ☐ out of the question   ☐ routine

The idea of being watched while we have sex is …
    ☐ appealing   ☐ not appealing   ☐ out of the question   ☐ routine

The idea of trying Tantric sex is …
    ☐ appealing   ☐ not appealing   ☐ out of the question   ☐ routine

The idea of trying phone sex is …
    ☐ appealing   ☐ not appealing   ☐ out of the question   ☐ routine

The idea of trying cybersex is …
    ☐ appealing   ☐ not appealing   ☐ out of the question   ☐ routine

The idea of photographing or videotaping ourselves having sex is …
    ☐ appealing   ☐ not appealing   ☐ out of the question   ☐ routine

The idea of trying bondage is …
    ☐ appealing   ☐ not appealing   ☐ out of the question   ☐ routine

The idea of trying light spanking is …
    ☐ appealing   ☐ not appealing   ☐ out of the question   ☐ routine

The idea of trying S&M is …
    ☐ appealing   ☐ not appealing   ☐ out of the question   ☐ routine

The idea of dressing up in leather or latex is …
    ☐ appealing   ☐ not appealing   ☐ out of the question   ☐ routine

The idea of trying group sex is …
    ☐ appealing   ☐ not appealing   ☐ out of the question   ☐ routine

The idea of swinging or joining a sex club is …
    ☐ appealing   ☐ not appealing   ☐ out of the question   ☐ routine

The idea of role playing is …
    ☐ appealing   ☐ not appealing   ☐ out of the question   ☐ routine

... And the most interesting roles for me would involve:
☐ military uniforms ☐ a French maid's outfit ☐ a stripper pole
☐ pizza delivery ☐ jungle loincloths ☐ doctors or nurses
☐ the old West ☐ a Sultan's harem ☐ the middle ages ☐ spacesuits
☐ other _____
☐ let's try em all!

The idea of experimenting with gender roles is …
☐ appealing ☐ not appealing ☐ out of the question ☐ routine

The idea of penetrating you with a sex toy is …
☐ appealing ☐ not appealing ☐ out of the question ☐ routine

The idea of you penetrating me with a sex toy is …
☐ appealing ☐ not appealing ☐ out of the question ☐ routine

The idea of having sex on an airplane is …
☐ appealing ☐ not appealing ☐ out of the question ☐ routine
☐ I'm a Mile-High Club frequent flier

My Foundation

chapter *4*

My Parents

My parents …
- ☐ stayed married, happily ☐ stayed married, unhappily
- ☐ divorced, amicably ☐ divorced, bitterly

The thing I liked most about my parents' (or parent and stepparent's) relationship is: _____

_____

The one thing in my relationships I'd never do like my parents did is:

_____

_____

My favorite thing to do with my dad when I was little was:

_____

_____

My favorite thing to do with my dad now is:

_____

_____

My favorite thing to do with my mom when I was little was:

_____

_____

My favorite thing to do with my mom now is:

_____

_____

When my parents were angry with me, they would:
☐ discuss it quietly ☐ yell ☐ hit ☐ give me a time-out
☐ give me the silent treatment ☐ other _____

When my parents were angry with each other, they would:
☐ hide it ☐ discuss it in normal speaking voices ☐ shout at each other
☐ fight physically ☐ other _____

My parents showed affection to each other in front of me by:
☐ saying nice things to each other ☐ holding hands or hugging ☐ kissing
☐ wrestling ☐ my parents didn't show physical affection to each other
☐ other _____

My parents showed physical affection to me by:
☐ hugging or kissing me in private ☐ hugging me in public
☐ playful wrestling or hair-tousling ☐ my parents didn't show physical
affection to me.

My mother told me she loved me:
☐ daily ☐ often ☐ seldom ☐ never

My father told me he loved me:
☐ daily ☐ often ☐ seldom ☐ never

The best trip I ever took with one or both of my parents was to:

_____

The best thing my mom did while raising me was:

_____
_____

The best thing my dad did while raising me was:

_____
_____

One thing my parents did that I'll never do to my kids was:

_____
_____

One thing I wish my parents had done for me is:

_____
_____

When I started dating, my parents were:
☐ overprotective ☐ too lenient ☐ just about right

My parents taught me about sex …
☐ early on ☐ way too late ☐ at about the right time

When my parents discussed love and sex with me, they were …
☐ frank and comfortable ☐ uncomfortable ☐ unwilling to talk
☐ they never discussed love and sex with me

My parents taught me that sex is …
☐ fun ☐ good and pleasurable ☐ dirty or bad
☐ only for married people ☐ only for procreation

I think that my parents …
☐ mostly approve of the way I handle my relationships
☐ mostly disapprove of the way I handle my relationships

… And that's:
☐ a good thing ☐ a bad thing ☐ not something I care about

Here's how I think my parents have shaped my attitudes toward relationships:

_____

_____

My Childhood

When I was a child, I loved to:
☐ play sports ☐ play board games ☐ make up stories ☐ play with dolls
☐ go exploring ☐ read ☐ well, actually what I most liked was to:

_____

The grandparent I was closest to: _____

Because: _____

_____

The subject in school I was best at: _____

The subject in school I was worst at: _____

My favorite teacher was: _____

The coolest thing I could draw was:

_____

I am…   ☐ an only child   ☐ one of two kids   ☐ one of many

If I was not an only child, I was …
☐ an older sister   ☐ a younger sister   ☐ a middle sister
☐ a stepsister or half-sister   ☐ an older brother   ☐ a younger brother.
☐ a middle brother   ☐ a stepbrother or a half-brother

I always wished I'd had …
☐ an older brother   ☐ a younger brother   ☐ an older sister
☐ a younger sister   ☐ more siblings in general   ☐ more space to myself
☐ none of these—I was perfectly happy

Okay, I'll admit it …
☐ as an only child, I still have trouble sharing
☐ as an older sibling, I still like to boss people around
☐ as a younger sibling, I'm still used to being taken care of
☐ as a middle sibling, I still feel like I have to fight for attention
☐ none of those, but I do have to admit that…

_____

When I was a kid, my favorite married or long-term couple was:

_____

One adult who encouraged me was: _____

One adult who discouraged me was: _____

If I could erase one thing an adult said to me when I was a kid, it would be:

_____
_____

The best thing an adult ever said to me when I was a kid:

_____
_____

My first pet's name: _____

My favorite pet: _____

My best friend as a child: _____

When I was a kid, I loved to pretend to be: _____

When I was a kid, I was sure I'd grow up to be: _____

When I was a kid, I was afraid of: _____

My favorite fairy tale or bedtime story was: _____

This made me feel safe because: _____

I practiced getting married as a kid.
   ☐ true   ☐ false

When I was a kid, I thought I'd marry: _____

My first childhood boyfriend or girlfriend was: _____

What I liked about him or her was:
_____

My first real boyfriend or girlfriend was: _____

What I liked about him or her was:
_____

My first real heartbreak was: _____

My biggest celebrity crush as an adolescent was on: _____

What I liked most about my crush was:
_____
_____

Here's how you remind me of my old crush:
_____
_____

I played doctor as a kid.
   ☐ yes, with friends of the same sex   ☐ yes, with friends of the opposite sex
   ☐ yes, with friends of both sexes   ☐ I never played doctor

I played spin the bottle, post office, or other kissing games …
   ☐ as a kid   ☐ in high school   ☐ in college   ☐ as an adult   ☐ never

In high school I was:
   ☐ a nerd   ☐ a mean girl   ☐ a jock   ☐ a cheerleader
   ☐ a class representative   ☐ a stoner   ☐ a punk   ☐ a goth
   ☐ a prep   ☐ a ghost   ☐ other _____

My Past

chapter 5

My Baggage

Three things I wish I'd done differently in my last relationship:

1. _____
2. _____
3. _____

Three things I wish my last partner had done differently:

1. _____
2. _____
3. _____

Looking back, I regret more …
☐ things I've done   ☐ things I haven't done

I've cheated on an ex and been caught.
☐ yes   ☐ no

I've cheated on an ex and gotten away with it.
☐ yes   ☐ no

My favorite thing that one of my exes used to do is:

_____

When I was a teenager, I'd date people whom …
☐ my parents liked   ☐ my parents disliked

I lost my virginity …
　　☐ in high school　☐ in college　☐ after leaving school
　　☐ before high school　☐ hasn't happened yet

I wish I'd …
　　☐ waited longer to lose my virginity
　　☐ lost it sooner
　　☐ I'm happy about the timing

Losing my virginity was …
　　☐ something I'd rather forget　☐ good emotionally, but not physically
　　☐ good physically, but not emotionally　☐ pretty great all around

The best sex I've ever had was:

_____
_____

The worst sex I've ever had was:

_____
_____

The most interesting place I've had sex was:

_____

The place I liked having sex the least was:

_____

I've had an STD.
　　☐ yes　☐ no

I've had an STD passed to me by accident.
　　☐ yes　☐ no

I've gotten an STD because my partner lied to me.
　　☐ yes　☐ no

I've been physically abused by an ex.
　　☐ yes　☐ no

I've been emotionally abused by an ex.
　　☐ yes　☐ no

I have been in a relationship where I felt like I was losing myself.
　　☐ yes　☐ no

Because:

_____

_____

I think I could have stopped that from happening by:

_____

The one relationship mistake I never want to repeat:

_____

_____

One thing an ex did that made it harder for me to trust people:

_____

_____

One thing an ex did that made it easier for me to trust people:

_____

_____

My favorite thing about you that reminds me of an ex:

_____

_____

My least favorite thing about you that reminds me of an ex:

_____

_____

The ex I took the longest time getting over: _____

Because: _____

_____

If I could go back in time and redo one thing from high school I'd:

_____

_____

If I could go back in time and redo one thing from college I'd:

_____

_____

If I had the choice to go back in time and say one thing I hadn't said or unsay one thing I had, I'd:

_____

_____

The biggest secret I hid under my bed as a teenager:

_____

Hiding under my bed now:

_____

MY WISDOM

The most important thing I learned about relationships in high school:

_____
_____

The most important thing I learned about relationships in my twenties:

_____
_____

The most important thing I've learned about relationships in the past year:

_____
_____

The most important thing I've learned about relationships with my current partner: _____
_____

The most important thing I've learned about relationships while I've been alone:

_____
_____

The most important thing I've learned from a past hurt:

_____
_____

The most important thing my parents taught me about relationships:

_____
_____

The most important thing I've learned about arguments:

_____
_____

The most important thing I've learned about sex:

_____
_____

The most important thing I've learned about attraction:

_____

_____

The most important thing I've learned about families:

_____

_____

The most important thing I've learned about you:

_____

_____

The most important thing I've learned about myself:

_____

_____

The area in which I feel like I still have the most to learn:

_____

_____

The best relationship advice I've ever gotten:

_____

_____

The best relationship advice I've ever given:

_____

_____

My Future

chapter 6

My Career

It's okay for me to put my career ahead of my partner.
☐ always ☐ sometimes ☐ never

It's okay for my partner's career to take precedence over me.
☐ always ☐ sometimes ☐ never

I'm willing to support my partner while he or she goes through school.
☐ yes ☐ no

I'm willing to drop my career to raise kids.
☐ yes, for a while ☐ yes, permanently ☐ no ☐ career?

I expect my partner to drop his or her career to raise kids.
☐ yes ☐ no

I'd prefer my partner to …
☐ be in the same field as me ☐ understand the field that I'm in
☐ be in a completely different field than me

I feel like you take my career seriously.
☐ true, and that's good ☐ true, and that's bad
☐ false, and that's good ☐ false, and that's bad

I feel like you think my job is …
- ☐ as important as yours ☐ more important than yours
- ☐ less important than yours

When it comes to my career …
- ☐ I'm right where I want to be
- ☐ I don't know what I want to do when I grow up
- ☐ I feel pressured to move faster
- ☐ I'm just doing this until something better comes along
- ☐ I feel like I'm ahead of the game
- ☐ I'd rather not work at all

If I won the lottery I'd …
- ☐ stop working altogether ☐ keep my job
- ☐ keep my line of work but start a new business
- ☐ launch a whole new career

The thing you could do that would be most helpful to my career would be:

_____

_____

I'll know I'm a success when:

_____

_____

In one year, I plan to be:

_____

_____

In five years, I plan to be:

_____

_____

In ten years, I plan to be:

_____

_____

In twenty years, I plan to be:

_____

_____

The difference between my career plans and my career dreams is:

_____

_____

Here's how you can help me lessen that difference:

_____

_____

If I could drop my current job and pursue any career at all, I'd:

_____

_____

The thing I like least about my job right now is:

_____

_____

The thing I like best about my job right now is:

_____

_____

MY HOME

I expect that …
- ☐ I'll be the disciplinarian ☐ you'll be the disciplinarian
- ☐ we'll share the job

I think it's okay to physically punish kids.
- ☐ yes ☐ only in extreme cases, such as slapping something dangerous out of a child's hand ☐ never

I expect any kids we have to be raised …
- ☐ within my specific branch of my faith ☐ with a religious foundation
- ☐ as agnostics ☐ as atheists

I expect that …
- ☐ you'll have the final say ☐ I'll have the final say
- ☐ we'll negotiate everything as a pair ☐ you'll always have the final word in some areas, I'll always have it in others

I expect that …
- ☐ you'll pay the bills ☐ I'll pay the bills
- ☐ we'll pay them together

I expect …
- ☐ your voice to be on our voicemail message
- ☐ my voice to be on our voicemail message
- ☐ both of us to be on our voicemail message

Speaking of that, I think that voicemail messages should be ...
☐ cute ☐ sexy ☐ straightforward ☐ funny

My home needs to be ...
☐ immaculate ☐ tidy
☐ pleasantly cluttered ☐ cleaned by others

My best roommate: _____

Because: _____
_____

My worst roommate: _____

Because: _____
_____

I have fixed a part of my home with the proper tools.
☐ true ☐ false

I'm like MacGyver with household problems. I just need a fork, a bobby pin, or some other surprisingly useful object.
☐ true ☐ false

I expect that household repairs or building projects will be ...
☐ done by you ☐ done by me
☐ done by the two of us
☐ done by skilled professionals

Here's how I think my home reflects my personality:
_____
_____

If I had to choose one, I'd like my home to look ...
☐ perfect, like a magazine
☐ lived-in

If I could change one thing about my home, I'd:
_____
_____

My favorite thing about my home is:
_____
_____

My favorite piece of furniture is:

_____

My favorite decoration in my home is:

_____

My favorite smell to have in my home is:

_____

If I could choose my perfect view, it would be:

_____

Day by Day

chapter 7

My Basics

I need to hear "I love you" every day.
  ☐ yes ☐ no

I like to have pet names for each other.
  ☐ yes ☐ no

I'd prefer you to introduce me as your …
  ☐ girlfriend/boyfriend ☐ friend ☐ lover ☐ reason for living

Calling each other at work to whisper sweet and/or filthy nothings is …
  ☐ childish ☐ fun ☐ unprofessional ☐ a good way to add spice

I'm comfortable with public displays of affection.
  ☐ yes ☐ no

The most intense public display of affection I'm comfortable with is …
  ☐ holding hands ☐ a peck on the cheek ☐ a closed-mouth kiss on the lips
  ☐ deep kissing ☐ heavy petting ☐ I haven't found my limit yet
  ☐ I'd prefer it if we just winked at each other

The most you should tell your friends about our sex life is …
  ☐ that it exists ☐ that we're dating ☐ tell them everything
  ☐ tell them nothing

I enjoy quickies.
  ☐ yes ☐ no

During sex, the lights should be …
  ☐ on ☐ off ☐ natural sunlight ☐ strobes and disco balls ☐ let's mix it up

Complaining about something that doesn't directly involve you means:
  ☐ I want you to solve it ☐ I just need to vent

I'm fine with eating dinner in front of the television.
　☐ yes ☐ no ☐ sometimes

I expect to spend big chunks of time with you …
　☐ daily ☐ weekly ☐ every now and then

How much time together is too much? _____

I sleep best …
　☐ alone ☐ when you're there, but on your own side
　☐ when we're spooning
　☐ in a great big tangle, possibly with a cat or dog thrown in

Food is …
　☐ one of life's sensual pleasures ☐ workout fuel ☐ a holistic way to
　　nourish and heal your body ☐ whatever comes out of the closest bag

If you're going to be out with your friends, I need you to call me and let me
know where you are …
　☐ always ☐ only if you need to change plans with me
　☐ only if you're going to be out late ☐ never

If you make plans for a night that's usually a date night, I need to be
informed …
　☐ as soon as possible ☐ sometime that day
　☐ not at all; I don't assume we have plans until we've made them

If you need to change plans we've made, I need to be told …
　☐ a week before ☐ at least a few hours before ☐ ten minutes before

It's okay for you to say that both of us will be going to a party without
checking with me first.
　☐ yes ☐ no
　☐ only if you know for sure I'll enjoy it and I don't already have plans

As a rule, I expect to have sex …
　☐ at least once a day ☐ at least once a week ☐ at least once or twice a
　　month ☐ at least once during the course of our relationship

When it comes to positions …
　☐ I'm strictly missionary ☐ I prefer to be on top
　☐ I like to switch it up between a few tried-and-true favorites and
　　something different for variety every now and then
　☐ I expect to discover at least six things that never made it into the
　　Kama Sutra

It's important to have moments of silence when we're together.
☐ definitely ☐ are you kidding me?

An evening in which we're both in the same room but doing different things is …
☐ perfect ☐ comfortable ☐ a sign that the relationship is in trouble

When I'm sad, I need to be …
☐ cheered up ☐ held
☐ commiserated with ☐ left alone

Masturbation is …
☐ a great way to show each other what we like in bed
☐ terrific, but only when we're alone
☐ something I've done, but am not comfortable with
☐ something I don't understand doing if we've got each other

A long-distance relationship …
☐ is out of the question ☐ would be difficult, but I could handle it
☐ is something I could do, but only for a year or less
☐ is something I could do, but only for six months or less
☐ sounds ideal

If you want to see a movie that I don't, and I want to see a movie that you don't, I expect that we will …
☐ see both movies together ☐ see our own movies separately
☐ it's more likely that we'll both see yours and not mine
☐ it's more likely that we'll both see mine and not yours

If it's one of the last two options above, here's what I think that says about our relationship: _____
_____

After sex, I like to:
☐ cuddle ☐ sleep ☐ shower ☐ watch TV ☐ talk
☐ other _____

I prefer to have sex …
☐ in the morning ☐ in the afternoon ☐ in the evening
☐ at night ☐ anytime, as long as we're having sex

It's okay to wake me up for sex.
☐ always ☐ never ☐ sometimes ☐ rarely

Sex should most often be:
☐ tender and comforting ☐ passionate and wild

Competing against you at games or sports is:
☐ fun ☐ okay, sometimes ☐ a bad idea

If one of us has dietary restrictions and one does not …
☐ all meals cooked by either of us should follow those restrictions
☐ the one with the restrictions follows them when cooking, the other
does not ☐ the one with the restrictions should occasionally cook
food that she or he can't or won't eat

If one of us is a vegetarian and one of us is not, it is okay for the carnivore
to keep beef jerky in the house.
☐ yes ☐ no

If at least one of us is a vegetarian, it is okay to feed house pets foods that
involve meat.
☐ yes ☐ no

Pets sleeping in bed with us is:
☐ disgusting ☐ cozy ☐ mandatory

Dogs should be …
☐ big and goofy ☐ big and fierce ☐ medium-sized
☐ easily concealed in the average purse
☐ purebred ☐ mutt

If there is a spider in the bathtub:
☐ you squash it ☐ I squash it ☐ you put it outside
☐ I put it outside ☐ what's the big deal?
☐ please don't ever make me think about spiders in the bathtub

Scooping out the chocolate chunks in the ice cream, leaving vanilla with
little tunnels in it:
☐ perfectly acceptable ☐ evil beyond all comprehension

Swearing is …
☐ okay, as long as it's not in public or in mixed company
☐ never acceptable ☐ acceptable if you save it for times when you're
genuinely upset ☐ fucking great

Spicy foods:
☐ the spice of life! ☐ too harsh

Breakfast should be:
☐ just coffee ☐ a quick bite of cereal or yogurt
☐ protein for my workout ☐ eggs, bacon, pancakes, the works!

Early to bed and early to rise makes a person …
☐ healthy, wealthy, and wise   ☐ irritating

In the car, I want to hear:
☐ silence ☐ us talking ☐ NPR/the news ☐ sports
☐ rock ☐ jazz ☐ classical ☐ books on tape

The maximum acceptable amount of TV watching per week is:
☐ unlimited ☐ anything under 20 hours ☐ anything under 10 hours
☐ anything under 5 hours ☐ anything

Following a TV series is:
☐ exciting and fun ☐ a waste of time

Talking about movies is:
☐ interesting ☐ a waste of time

Talking about movie stars is:
☐ interesting ☐ a waste of time

Talking about sports is:
☐ interesting ☐ kill me

My Friends and Family

I expect you to know the names of and basic information about my friends.
☐ no ☐ only my closest circle ☐ all of them

I expect you to know the names of and basic information about …
☐ my parents ☐ my parents and siblings
☐ parents, siblings, grandparents and cousins
☐ we're going to be getting into second and third cousins, so brace
yourself

It's important for me to spend holidays with my family.
☐ yes ☐ no

The idea of having sex with you in my parents' house over a holiday is …
☐ naughty fun ☐ ordinary ☐ never speak of it again

The member of my family I get along best with is: _____

The member of my family I think I'm most like is: _____

The member of my family I'd most like to improve my relationship with is:

_____

I have … ☐ a few close friends ☐ lots of acquaintances

Three things I see in my friends' relationships that I hope won't happen to us:
1. _____
2. _____
3. _____

Three things I envy about my friends' relationships:
1. _____
2. _____
3. _____

My best friend: _____

My best opposite-sex friend (if different): _____

The friend who is the worst influence on me: _____

The friend I most admire: _____

The first friend I'd call in a crisis: _____

The friend I'd want on my side in a physical fight: _____

The friend with the juiciest secrets: _____

The friend I'd most like to trade lives with: _____

The friend I'd never trade lives with: _____

The friend I most wish I'd kept in touch with: _____

The friend I'm most competitive with: _____

The friend I think you're most attracted to: _____

The friend I think is most likely to make a pass at you: _____

The friend you are most irrationally jealous of: _____

The friend I'm secretly attracted to: _____

If I had to marry one of my best same-sex friends I'd choose:

_____

Because: _____
_____

I've dumped someone because of my friends.
☐ true   ☐ false

I've dated someone because of my friends
☐ true   ☐ false

I've stolen a mate from a friend.
☐ true   ☐ false

I've had a friend steal a mate from me.
☐ true   ☐ false

The worst friendship breakup I've had was:

_____
_____

The most touching thing a friend ever did for me was:

_____
_____

MY FINANCES

I expect:
☐ my partner to take care of me   ☐ to take care of my partner
☐ to trade off, depending on who's doing well

I'm in debt.
☐ no way   ☐ a little
☐ a lot   ☐ I'm drowning

It's okay for my partner to be in debt.
☐ yes, unreservedly   ☐ yes, for things like student loans
☐ depends on the partner, the kind, and the amount   ☐ not at all

Once we're married or living together, I expect us to have …
☐ separate bank accounts   ☐ joint bank accounts
☐ your account, my account, and our account

I'd prefer ...
☐ for you to take a strong interest in my finances ☐ for you to have a general idea of how I'm getting along ☐ for each of us to just take care of our own

Prenuptial agreements are:
☐ smart planning ☐ appalling

Making major purchases without telling each other is ...
☐ okay ☐ not okay

I expect to be ...
☐ richer than my parents ☐ less well-off than my parents ☐ about the same

I expect that ...
☐ I will make more money ☐ you will make more money ☐ it will be about the same ☐ I will make all the money ☐ you will make all the money

In all honesty, I would lose a little respect for my partner if I were the bigger breadwinner.
☐ true ☐ false

I'm a ...
☐ saver ☐ spender ☐ it feels like a pretty even balance

Ideally, I feel like I should be paired with a ...
☐ saver ☐ spender ☐ it doesn't matter

I feel like I'm prepared for retirement.
☐ yes ☐ no ☐ I've done some planning, but could do more ☐ what?

My Quirks

I care about whether the toilet paper rolls over or under.
☐ yes ☐ no

I need to be able to sleep on "my" side of the bed.
☐ yes ☐ no

Love me, love my pet.
☐ negotiable ☐ nonnegotiable

My living space needs to be …
- ☐ immaculate ☐ tidy, but not pristine
- ☐ cluttered, but sanitary ☐ left alone

Tidying my stuff away for me would be …
- ☐ helpful ☐ a violation ☐ not something I'd notice

Toothpaste tube:
- ☐ squeeze from the bottom and roll up carefully
- ☐ grab and squeeze from the middle ☐ toothpaste?

Being alone is:
- ☐ something I need so I can recharge ☐ horrible

Three things I suspect might bug you about me:
1. _____
2. _____
3. _____

I have eliminated someone as a potential date because of a bad voicemail.
- ☐ true ☐ false

My top three pet peeves:
1. _____
2. _____
3. _____

I think it's rude when people:

_____

My favorite thing is when I notice people:

_____

My favorite little courtesy:

_____

Three things I pretend I like more than I actually do:
1. _____
2. _____
3. _____

Three things I pretend I like less than I actually do:
1. _____
2. _____
3. _____

My Body

CARE AND FEEDING

Working out is …
- ☐ my life ☐ something I do, but dislike
- ☐ something I avoid at all costs

Plastic surgery is:
- ☐ creepy ☐ a miracle

For me, personal grooming is …
- ☐ the basics—a shower and a touch-up ☐ my favorite part of the day
- ☐ something I'll go all-out on for special occasions
- ☐ an hour in the bathroom every morning, minimum

You can expect to see me wearing makeup …
- ☐ most days, because that's what's expected of women in our culture
- ☐ most days, because I feel better wearing it ☐ on special occasions
- ☐ grudgingly ☐ if you have a gun to my head

I consider myself …
- ☐ a vegetarian ☐ a carnivore ☐ a vegan
- ☐ health-conscious ☐ can't people just be quiet and eat?

I have dietary restrictions …
- ☐ due to my religion ☐ due to allergies ☐ due to a health issues
- ☐ due to moral issues ☐ for weight control
- ☐ my diet is only restricted by the capacity of my stomach

I can live with someone who has dietary restrictions that are different than mine …
- ☐ unreservedly ☐ begrudgingly ☐ if they're for health reasons
- ☐ if they're for religious or moral reasons ☐ I can't live with someone who has dietary restrictions different than mine

I prefer my underarms …
- ☐ shaved ☐ natural

I prefer my legs …
- ☐ shaved ☐ natural

I prefer to keep my pubic region …
- ☐ natural ☐ trimmed ☐ partially shaved or waxed ☐ bare

If you have a different preference …
- ☐ I'll keep it the way you like it best
- ☐ we can discuss it, depending on what you want
- ☐ you should think about whether that's a dealbreaker for you

I have an injury, so during sex it hurts me when you put too much pressure on or are too rough with my:

_____

Yoga is:
- ☐ good for the body ☐ good for the body, mind and spirit ☐ no good

MIND OVER MATTER

My favorite body part is: _____

My least favorite body part is: _____

I think I look best when I'm:

_____

I feel sexiest when I'm:

_____

I don't like it when you touch my: _____

I love it when you touch my: _____

I think the sex symbol I'm most like is: _____

The sex symbol I've never understood the appeal of is: _____

Here's the advantage I have over him or her:

_____

The most attractive I've been in my life is:

_____

_____

I know I can always seduce you by:

_____

_____

I'm pretty sure I could seduce anyone by:

_____

_____

Dancing makes me feel …
☐ sexy   ☐ self-conscious

I forget to be self-conscious when I'm:

_____

I think I'm …
☐ great in bed   ☐ average in bed
☐ in need of some practice and maybe a manual or two

The best thing you could say to me before sex is:

_____

_____

The best thing you could say to me after sex is:

_____

_____

The best thing you could say to me during sex is:

_____

_____

Fighting Words

chapter **9**

In the Heat of the Moment

If I'm upset about something, I need to talk about it …
☐ right now ☐ after I've cooled down

Fights are …
☐ best avoided at all costs ☐ exciting ☐ scary
☐ over the minute one of us uses a raised voice
☐ a useful way to hash out issues ☐ no holds barred

If you ask me if something is wrong and I say "nothing," I really want you to …
☐ pursue me and dig a little deeper ☐ leave me alone while I think about it
☐ believe me when I say that there's nothing wrong

Things you say to me during the course of an argument are …
☐ brushed off the minute we're done ☐ going to keep hurting for a while

Going to bed angry:
☐ never ☐ sometimes you just have to

All fights need to be resolved before they're dropped.
☐ yes ☐ no

A fight about doing the dishes is …
☐ probably about doing the dishes ☐ probably about something else

Bringing up past arguments in a current fight:
☐ fair ☐ unfair

A couple that never fights is …
　☐ happy ☐ suppressing things

Taking a break in the middle of a fight to cool down is …
　☐ a good idea ☐ not something I can do

I expect …
　☐ one of us to win the fight ☐ the two of us to compromise

You have hit a level of anger that frightens me in the past.
　☐ yes ☐ no

I have hit a level of anger that frightened me in the past.
　☐ yes ☐ no

I prefer to discuss problems in our relationship …
　☐ face to face ☐ while we're doing something else, like taking a walk
　☐ with someone else first

After a fight, I need to …
　☐ be apart for a while
　☐ connect with you right away, to know we're okay

We fight …
　☐ more than I did in most past relationships ☐ less than I did in most
　past relationships ☐ about the same

The thing you do during arguments that I find unfair is:

_____

The thing I do during arguments that is probably unfair is:

_____

I wish you had more of a sense of humor about:

_____

That said, I am never going to have a sense of humor about:

_____

I think we resolve conflicts:
　☐ well ☐ badly

Talking to friends about our fights:
　☐ okay ☐ not okay

Relationship counselors …
☐ help couples argue more productively   ☐ don't help

The one fight I'd love to remove from our lives together is:

_____

We're going to have to agree to disagree about:

_____

The dumbest fight we've had was about:

_____

The fight that was best for our relationship was:

_____

Brutally Honest

Really, honestly, truly—relationship drama is …
☐ something I can't stand
☐ something I might secretly enjoy a little bit
☐ my lifeblood

I'm likely to say something I don't mean in a fight.
☐ true   ☐ false

I am able to admit it when I'm in the wrong.
☐ yes   ☐ no   ☐ yes, but usually not right away

I'm used to winning arguments.
☐ true   ☐ false

Makeup sex:
☐ no such thing   ☐ depends on the fight
☐ the whole reason for having the argument in the first place

I've resorted to emotional blackmail before.
☐ true   ☐ false

Withholding sex to get my way is …
☐ fair   ☐ unfair
☐ unfair, but I'll do it if it's something important to me

Breaking Up

chapter

Water Under the Bridge

I have more often been …
☐ the one who gets dumped ☐ the one who does the dumping
☐ it's about even

In the past, I have threatened to break up …
☐ in the heat of an argument
☐ if it's an issue that's really important to me
☐ only when I am actually prepared to walk out the door
☐ I don't threaten, I do it

The one thing I couldn't stand about my worst breakup was:

_____
_____
_____
_____

The thing I most appreciated a partner doing in a past breakup was:

_____
_____
_____
_____

Breaking up in a restaurant or other public place in the hopes that the other person won't make a scene:
☐ fair ☐ unfair

Breakups should happen:

☐ in person   ☐ on the phone   ☐ via text message
☐ just do "the fade" and stop calling

In the past, I've waited until I found a new partner before breaking up with the old one.

☐ true   ☐ false

The thing that worries me most about your past breakups:

_____
_____
_____

The worst thing I did in a past breakup:

_____
_____
_____

The thing I'm proudest of in handling a past breakup:

_____
_____
_____

A Little Too Close for Comfort

I've thought about leaving my current relationship.

☐ true   ☐ false

I thought about leaving because:

_____
_____
_____

I ended up staying because:

_____
_____
_____

I sometimes worry about your tendency to:

_____
_____
_____

If we ever break up, I expect it to be because of:

_____

_____

_____

How to Win Me

chapter *11*

The Chase

I'd rather …
- ☐ be pursued   ☐ do the pursuing

Someone who is openly attracted to me is …
- ☐ an aphrodisiac   ☐ too easy

I'm intrigued by people who challenge me.
- ☐ yes   ☐ no

I'd rather have you …
- ☐ seduce me with your eyes from across the room
- ☐ slam me into a wall and kiss me hard

I prefer …
- ☐ to know you're making an effort to charm me
- ☐ for you to be absolutely real with me

Witty banter:
- ☐ is the spice of life   ☐ requires too much thought

I still enjoy a high school–style makeout in the back of a car
- ☐ true   ☐ false

Tickling:
- ☐ love it   ☐ hate it   ☐ not ticklish

Teasing me:
☐ love it ☐ hate it

Teasing me in bed:
☐ love it ☐ hate it

A bubble bath for two sounds …
☐ sensual ☐ crowded

Soft music and candlelight is …
☐ romantic ☐ boring ☐ fun to try

Foot rubs are ...
☐ good ☐ weird ☐ best when they lead to something more

I'd rather …
☐ be the boss ☐ be dominated a little bit ☐ switch roles

Staring into each others' eyes during sex:
☐ intimate ☐ creepy

The Cold Hard Truth

In all honesty, physical attractiveness is …
☐ irrelevant ☐ a nice icing on the cake
☐ something that makes me a little wary ☐ one way to attract me
☐ the main thing I look for ☐ essential

In all honesty, sending me mixed signals …
☐ turns me off ☐ intrigues me

In all honesty, I tend to be more attracted to people who don't quite treat me well.
☐ true ☐ false ☐ true, but I'm trying to break the habit

In all honesty, sexual prowess is …
☐ essential ☐ icing on the cake ☐ a little too much pressure

In all honesty, if you stop chasing me …
☐ we can relax ☐ I'll leave

In all honesty, a little danger in the relationship is …
☐ essential ☐ going to drive me away eventually

In all honesty, sexual variety is …
　☐ essential　☐ exhausting

In all honesty, I need to date someone who is taller than me.
　☐ true　☐ false

In all honesty, I need to date someone who is taller than me when I wear heels.
　☐ true　☐ false

In all honesty, I need to be with someone who has a higher income than me.
　☐ true　☐ false

In all honesty, I need to be with someone who has a lower income than me.
　☐ true　☐ false

In all honesty, making me a little jealous is a good way to keep me interested.
　☐ true　☐ false

In all honesty, I'm really only fully attracted to …
　☐ someone who takes on a strong masculine role
　☐ someone who takes on a strong feminine role
　☐ someone who completely rejects traditional masculinity
　☐ someone who completely rejects traditional femininity
　☐ someone who's a little androgynous
　☐ I'm flexible

How to Spoil Me

chapter *12*

Spoil Little

Surprises make me feel …
☐ happy and excited ☐ anxious and out of control

Giving me a romantic card "just because" is …
☐ sweet ☐ sappy

A nice massage …
☐ puts me to sleep ☐ turns me on
☐ there is no such thing as a nice massage

Breakfast in bed should be …
☐ eggs and sausage ☐ pancakes ☐ fresh berries and cream ☐ all of those
☐ avoided until I've had a chance to wash my face and brush my teeth

Lingerie is …
☐ really a gift for me ☐ really a gift for you

Giving me a book as a present is …
☐ thoughtful ☐ good, depending on the book
☐ the same as giving me a doorstop

Lotions and bath salts are …
☐ in the way ☐ luxurious

A single rose:
☐ the perfect romantic gesture ☐ where are the rest of them?

Surprising me after work with a movie rental and some takeout is …
☐ a relaxing treat ☐ a little too much like our usual routine

The best thing you can do for me after I've had a hard day at work is …
☐ cook me dinner ☐ give me a back rub ☐ leave me alone for a while
☐ give me a hug ☐ let me talk about it

If you were to cook (or buy) me a meal, I'd like:

_____

I think that Valentine's Day is …
☐ romantic ☐ silly, but fun ☐ something we should ignore
☐ mandatory

Flowers or Valentine presents delivered to my office are …
☐ fun, but unnecessary ☐ embarrassing ☐ a sweet gesture
☐ a way to rack up major points

My birthday is …
☐ something I prefer to ignore ☐ something I celebrate privately
☐ a great excuse to go out drinking with friends
☐ a night for a party and cake ☐ ME DAY

It's okay to give me a gift that's really for my child or my pet for my birthday.
☐ true ☐ false

Birthday and holiday presents should be …
☐ practical ☐ fun ☐ complete surprises

Writing me a poem or song is …
☐ incredibly romantic ☐ sweet, but not my thing

Spoil Big

The perfect weekend morning for me is …
☐ work ☐ going to religious services
☐ a quiet breakfast in bed ☐ reading the paper, cover to cover
☐ yoga, a bike ride, or a hike at sunrise ☐ over before I wake up

Giving me a spa day would …
☐ make me feel pampered ☐ make me feel like you think I need work

Public displays such as having musicians in a restaurant come over to
serenade me are …
☐ wonderful! ☐ embarrassing, but fun
☐ the perfect way to drive me under the table

The idea of a whole night dedicated just to my pleasure …
☐ makes me nervous ☐ makes me feel selfish
☐ sounds wonderful if I can reciprocate later ☐ sounds perfect

If I could visit any country in the world, I'd choose: _____

A vacation to me means …
  ☐ lots of physical activity ☐ lots of relaxing

A camping trip sounds like …
  ☐ a lot of fun ☐ you're testing me and our relationship
  ☐ most of my long weekends ☐ pure hell

A weekend getaway should be …
  ☐ just us ☐ us and our friends

Assuming kids are in the picture, I'd prefer …
  ☐ romantic vacations for two ☐ family vacations

The perfect vacation spot for me would be …
  ☐ anyplace with plenty of booze, clubs and dancing ☐ anyplace with a
  beach ☐ international city, glamorous hotel, plenty of shopping
  ☐ a cottage in the country ☐ a tent in the woods ☐ anyplace I can get
  some extreme sports in ☐ backpacking through a country I've never
  been to ☐ my place, with the phone turned off

Perfume is …
  ☐ a good present because I want to wear a scent you like
  ☐ not a good present unless you already know what I prefer to wear
  ☐ a good present because you chose it for me
  ☐ not a good present because I don't like perfume

Diamonds are …
  ☐ a waste of money ☐ a girl's best friend ☐ immoral
  ☐ pretty, but not necessary ☐ something I'd enjoy

Should it come up, I'd rather …
  ☐ be surprised with a ring ☐ shop together

It makes me feel like a princess when you …

_____

I've always dreamed of living in a:
  ☐ penthouse apartment ☐ castle ☐ mansion
  ☐ little house with a yard ☐ igloo ☐ tree house ☐ yacht
  ☐ other _____

More Things to Love about Me

chapter *13*

My Likes and Dislikes

My favorite movie: _____

My favorite book: _____

My favorite children's book: _____

My favorite guilty television pleasure: _____

You're never going to get me to eat: _____

The habit that drives me crazy:

_____

My favorite sport to watch: _____

My favorite sport to play: _____

My favorite game that I'm good at: _____

My favorite game that I'm bad at: _____

My favorite city: _____

My favorite vacation spot: _____

The country I'd most like to live in: _____

My favorite band: _____

My favorite sound: _____

My favorite smell: _____

My most hated smell: _____

My favorite actor: _____

My favorite actress: _____

My favorite comedian/comedienne: _____

My favorite classy celebrity: _____

My favorite trashy celebrity: _____

My favorite drink: _____

My favorite season: _____

My favorite word: _____

My favorite color: _____

My favorite gift I've received as an adult: _____

My favorite childhood gift: _____

My favorite family member: _____

My favorite body part on men: _____

My favorite body part on women: _____

My favorite song right now: _____

My favorite song of all time: _____

My favorite sad song: _____

My favorite love song: _____

My favorite rock-out song: _____

My favorite makeout song: _____

My favorite karaoke song: _____

My favorite CD: _____

My favorite thing I've made with my hands: _____

My favorite way to travel:
    ☐ road trip ☐ plane ☐ ocean liner ☐ bike
    ☐ there's no place like home ☐ other _____

My favorite kind of party:
    ☐ swanky cocktails ☐ dinner for six
    ☐ plenty of friends, plenty of board games ☐ loud music and sexy dancing
    ☐ other _____

My favorite night at the movies:
    ☐ romance ☐ suspense ☐ comedy ☐ action ☐ horror ☐ foreign
    ☐ documentary ☐ other _____

I prefer to wear:
    ☐ high heels ☐ sneakers ☐ slippers ☐ flip-flops ☐ other _____

INSIDE MY HEAD

Three things about me of which I'm proudest:
    1. _____
    2. _____
    3. _____

Three things about me that are the hardest to admit:
    1. _____
    2. _____
    3. _____

The quality I see in myself that I can't stand in others is:

_____

I know way too much about: _____

The best compliment I've ever received:

_____

The weirdest compliment I've ever received:

_____

The one thing that always turns me off is:

_____

The fantasy that's always secretly turned me on is:

_____

The movie scene that never fails to get me going is:

_____

Before I met you, of course, the person who used to pop into my head
while I was masturbating was: _____

Making noise in bed …
    ☐ adds spice   ☐ makes me worry we'll be overheard
    ☐ makes me worry that I'll sound silly   ☐ is essential

The oldest person I've fantasized about: _____

The youngest person I've fantasized about: _____

I fantasize more about …
    ☐ being rescued   ☐ doing the rescuing

To me, the sexiest profession is …
    ☐ firefighter   ☐ doctor   ☐ mechanic   ☐ CEO   ☐ construction worker
    ☐ lawyer   ☐ police officer   ☐ artist   ☐ international spy   ☐ actor
    ☐ other _____

I'd rather …
    ☐ see something sexy   ☐ read something sexy   ☐ hear something sexy

I believe sexual orientation is …
    ☐ fixed   ☐ fluid

The best dream I ever had is:

_____
_____

I think it means:

_____
_____

If I could change one thing about the world right now, I'd:

_____

The girliest thing about me is:

_____

The most boyish thing about me is:

_____

JUST FOR FUN

I've always wished I were really good at:

_____

The surefire way to make me laugh is to:

_____

The surest way to tell that I'm happy is:

_____

The best indication that I need some space is:

_____

My weirdest celebrity crush is: _____

I think I'd have made a good ...
- ☐ princess ☐ empress ☐ pirate ☐ comedian ☐ rock star
- ☐ Amazon ☐ saucy maid ☐ spy

My inner animal is a: _____

If I were a drink, I would be a . . .
- ☐ soda ☐ juice ☐ beer ☐ martini ☐ white wine ☐ red wine
- ☐ gin and tonic ☐ scotch ☐ other _____

If I were a kind of flower, I would be: _____

If I could choose my own nickname, I'd pick: _____

If I were making lunch or dinner to please my inner child, I'd make:

_____

The fairy-tale character I most identify with: _____

My favorite real-life hero: _____

My favorite superhero: _____

The villain I secretly identify with: _____

The public figure I'm convinced is a real-life villain: _____

The era in history I'd most like to live in: _____

If I could go back in time and change one historical event, it would be:

_____

I know it's not the height of fashion, but I love the way I look when I wear my:

_____

If I could put a multiple murderer behind bars, but I'd have to enter the Witness Protection Program and never see my friends and family again, I'd:

_____

The worst thing I personally have done:

_____

_____

My biggest fear:

_____

_____

If I could have one superpower I'd choose: _____

If I could choose one micropower I'd choose:
- ☐ always being able to find a parking space
- ☐ waking up on time without an alarm clock
- ☐ a personal radius of perfect cell phone reception
- ☐ other _____

If I could be a genius at one art form I'd choose:
- ☐ classical musician ☐ rock star ☐ jazz cat ☐ painter ☐ sculptor
- ☐ architect ☐ actor ☐ singer ☐ dancer ☐ photographer ☐ director
- ☐ writer ☐ other _____

I think the game show I'd be most likely to clean up on is: _____

A reality show about my life would be called: _____

The worst haircut I've ever had was:

_____

I'd rather win:
- ☐ an Olympic medal ☐ a Nobel prize

If I could eradicate one disease, I'd knock out: _____

If I had to pick just one or the other, I'd take:

☐ more smarts	☐ increased hotness
☐ master thief	☐ master sleuth
☐ caviar	☐ chili dog
☐ Brad Pitt	☐ Cary Grant
☐ cheese	☐ chocolate
☐ knight in shining armor	☐ scruffy dude on a Harley
☐ Oscar Wilde	☐ The Three Stooges
☐ James Bond	☐ Indiana Jones
☐ Wonder Woman	☐ Xena: Warrior Princess
☐ fruit	☐ vegetables
☐ King Kong	☐ Godzilla
☐ pink	☐ black
☐ Glinda the Good Witch	☐ The Wicked Witch of the West
☐ pirate	☐ ninja
☐ leather	☐ lace
☐ Broadway musical	☐ basketball game
☐ walking	☐ sprinting
☐ Abba	☐ The Sex Pistols
☐ music with a message	☐ shut up and dance

I am a ...
☐ cat person ☐ dog person ☐ person who thinks it's ridiculous to try
to divide the world into cat people and dog people

In the movie of my life, I'd be played by: _____

Psychics:
☐ valuable insight into the spirit world ☐ silly fun
☐ complete frauds

I believe in ghosts.
☐ true ☐ false

The most high-maintenance thing I do is:

_____
_____

The possession I'd run into a burning building to save:

_____

I keep a diary.
☐ yes ☐ no

If I knew I could get away with it, the biggest crime I'd commit is:

_____

I'm embarrassed about this, but I'm really good at:

_____

The coolest thing on my iPod:

_____

The most embarrassing thing on my iPod:

_____

One last awesome thing you need to know about me:

_____

_____

_____

_____

About the Author

Ali Davis has worked as a freelance writer and copyeditor for more than ten years. Her humor essays have been published in *Salon*, *Swivel*, and *Fresh Yarn*, and appeared on NPR's *This American Life*. Ali also writes personal quizzes for Lifetimetv.com and Beliefnet.org, and is the author of *True Porn Clerk Stories*, one of the first blogs to reach more than one million hits. Ali lives in New York, NY.